ccm *l i f e* L I N E S

Copyright © 2000 by CCM Books, a division of CCM Communications

Published by Harvest House Publishers, Eugene, Oregon 97402

Library of Congress Cataloging-in-Publication Data

Riddle, Melissa.
    Steven Curtis Chapman / by Melissa Riddle.
        p. cm. – (CCM lifelines)
    Discography: p.
    ISBN 0-7369-0272-4
      1. Chapman, Steven Curtis. 2. Singers—United States—Biography. 3. Contemporary
Christian musicians—United States—Biography. I. Title. II. Series.

ML420.C4537 RS3 2000
782.421640'92—dc21
[B]

                                                  99-057613

Printed in the United States of America.

00 01 02 03 04 05 / IP / 10 9 8 7 6 5 4 3 2 1

First Edition

Steven Curtis Chapman is managed by Dan Raines/David Huffman, Creative Trust, Inc., Nashville, Tennessee
Steven Curtis Chapman is booked by John Huie, Creative Artists Agency, Nashville, Tennessee

A publication of CCM Creative Ventures • Writer: Melissa Riddle • **Art Direction & Design:** Susan Browne; Susan Browne Design • **Cover Photograph:** Matthew Barnes • **Interior Photographs:** Robert Fleischauer, Matthew Barnes

STEVEN CURTIS CHAPMAN

stevencurtischapman

STEVEN
CURTIS
CHAPMAN

IS ARGUABLY THE MOST SUC-CESSFUL, MOST HIGHLY REGARDED CONTEMPORARY CHRISTIAN ARTIST TO EVER SET FOOT ON A STAGE. FROM HIS RECORDING DEBUT WITH

First Hand in 1987, he has dominated the Gospel Music Association's Dove Awards, winning 38, more than any other artist in history. He has had more number one songs on the Christian charts than any other artist of the decade—32 in all. He has won three Grammy Awards, six of his albums have been certified gold and one platinum. He has toured hundreds of cities in the U.S. and has performed abroad in over 30 countries.

And yet, what most people who've ever come in

SCC IN '63

The beginning
of the Great
Adventure!

Mom was left speechless by her little charmer!

contact with Steven Curtis Chapman—whether in person, at a concert, or through the pages of a magazine—remember most is not the face or the awards or even the music. When most people think of Steven Curtis, they think of him as simply one of the nicest guys they've ever met. No ego. No pretense. No attitude. Just a nice guy. An incredibly talented musician and songwriter, sure.

But more importantly, a really nice guy.

SIGNS OF LIFE

gnsoflifesignsoflifesignsof

"*I drew my first breath*

one cold November morning

and before my feet had

even touched the ground,

I started to dance..."

FROM "LORD OF THE DANCE" ON *SIGNS OF LIFE*, 1997

THE

EARLY

YEARS

Born in Paducah, Kentucky, on November 21, 1962, Steven Curtis Chapman entered the world as a nice guy, a good Kentucky boy. His parents' marriage wasn't perfect, but they worked at building a strong, if not always peaceful, home for their sons. His mother, Judy, was a stay-at-home mom, her hands full with baby Steven and his 3-year-old brother, Herb Jr.

Steven's father, Herb Sr., was a songwriter and musician who gave up the possibility of a country music career to be a "present and accounted for" husband and dad. "I remember that he sat down with some people who worked with Elvis when he began, and they told him they could make him a star. They said, 'But here's what you have to do: If your contract says to do 350 dates a year, that's what you'll do. If you're

BROTHER ACT

Stevie and Herbie's early career.

Herb Chapman Sr., Proprietor, Chapman Music
Located in the garage of Steven's boyhood home in Paducah, Kentucky.

sick and can't stand up and this says you'll be on stage, you'll be on stage.'

Dad looked at that [contract] and realized it would be his life and that

he'd have no family life," Steven has said.

During the day, Herb Sr. ran a music store in town. At night, he

wrote songs. And from the time Steven was old enough to toddle about

the house, he was interested in the sounds that his dad and his dad's

friends were strumming up in the kitchen behind closed doors. On

Saturday nights, dad and friends would perform folk, bluegrass and

country music around Paducah, the sounds of which would stay with

Steven well into adulthood.

By the time Steven was six years old, he had logged many an hour in his dad's store, until finally, at long last, he was given a guitar of his own. He picked it up quite naturally, and within a year began to accompany his brother, Herb, who sang Christian and popular cover songs at such exciting gigs as elementary school talent shows and musicals, civic meetings and church events. The Chapman boys made big impressions wherever they went.

And as Steven moved upward in school, he worked even harder at making a good impression on his peers and teachers. He found the divisions between the kids in school discouraging, and made a real effort to be well liked by the "cool kids" and the "not so cool kids" alike. It was a rare feat indeed, but Steven managed to befriend so many of his peers, that he was named "Mr. Concord," which is to say the most popular, and certainly the nicest, boy in elementary school.

Through the example of faith his parents had shown him, having recently rededicated their lives to Christ, Steven gave his own life to Jesus at the tender age of eight. "I remember being in church one Sunday

morning and just knowing that the Lord was calling me, that He was knocking on the door of my heart," Steven says. "I went forward and accepted Christ, and it was a very real commitment."

LITTLE LEAGUER

Even back in Paducah, Steven was ready for all the hits coming his way!

Steven and Herbie continued to play and sing together throughout the middle school and junior high years. "I Believe in Music" and "Try a Little Kindness" could work wonders with a crowd. But Christian artists such as Dallas Holm and Second Chapter of Acts, and mainstream artists such as The Doobie Brothers and Jim Croce tremendously influenced Steven, who had begun to teach himself to play piano and write his own songs. "As I grew older," Steven says, "I began to feel an emptiness when I would play anything other than something that would last beyond people just enjoying themselves." Steven began devoting all his songwriting attention to Christian music.

And as sure as the tide rolls in and out, change happens. Herbie went off to college, leaving people who knew the Chapman brothers' act to wonder what Steven would do with his talent now that Herbie was gone. His first solo gig was anything but a smash. With knees knocking, he sang four or five songs at a swimming pool luau and then ran off stage, a nervous wreck.

As God would have it, Steven got a summer job at Opryland USA in Nashville the summer before his freshman year at Georgetown College in

Kentucky. While there he would meet Danny

Daniels, a piano player for Danny Gaither, Bill

Gaither's brother. Steven became fast friends

with Danny, and they would get together on

23

weekends to rehearse.

Danny began to show some of Steven's songs to his boss' famous brother and encouraged Steven to transfer from Georgetown to Anderson University (home of the Gaithers and others in Christian music). With the encouragement from family and friends, and a whole lot of prayer, Steven did just that, changing his major from pre-medicine to music business. Soon enough his songs were in demand by people such as The Imperials, Dallas Holm, Dion, and rising new artist, Sandi Patty.

Within another year and a half, Steven had transferred schools again, this time to Belmont College in Nashville, which had a strong music program. He continued to sharpen his performance skills on the Opryland stage in the summer. Within yet another two years, Steven signed an exclusive publishing and recording agreement with Sparrow Records, a place where he could finally write and sing his own songs, in his own way.

College had done a lot more for Steven than give him an education. So much more than that.

What was the name of the Christian rock band Steven started in his teens?

TRIVIA QUESTION

PEACE

THE GREAT ADVENTURE

egreatadventurethegreat

"*I will be here.*

You can cry on my shoulder.

When the mirror tells us

we're older,

I will hold you..."

FROM "I WILL BE HERE" ON *MORE TO THIS LIFE* (1989)

THE
CHAPMAN
FAMILY PLAN

Steven Curtis and Mary Beth shared a mailbox on campus at Anderson College, oddly enough because both their last names were Chapman. But they didn't actually meet until the semester was well under way. Unknown to them, that mailbox was just the beginning of a lifetime of sharing. They began

["And she loved me for who I was, not what I did. And that was how I loved her too."]

dating, classic Christian college style: escorted walks to class, Steven's planned "accidental" meetings. Their first official date almost never happened. Steven was two hours late, a telltale sign of the life that was to come. Even so, Mary Beth would often wind up listening to Steven writing songs until the wee hours of the morning, falling asleep on the music room floor (and not because the songs were snoozers). They fell in love, and as Steven puts it, "marrying Mary Beth was never a question of if, but when....I wasn't Steven Curtis Chapman then. I wasn't a star. I was just Steve Chapman, a kid who sat in college rehearsal room and wrote songs. And she loved me for who I was, not what I did. And that was how I loved her too." The *when* was October 10, 1984, sooner rather than later.

The whirlwind only intensified during their first year of marriage. Two college kids, struggling to come to a realistic understanding of what it means to be married, making all the adjustments and putting aside the fantasy. "We had to figure out what to do with our disappointment, when the fairy tale isn't what we thought it would be," Steven says, reflecting on his and Mary Beth's initiation into marriage. "We had as many misconceptions as anybody could about what marriage is ultimately for. We were really young, and it was volatile at times." But the young couple was determined, despite the adjustment, to stick it out.

Less than a year into marriage, Mary Beth became pregnant with Emily as Steven's music career was beginning to take off. More adjustments.

stevencurtischapman

[
"We had as many misconceptions
as anybody could about what
marriage is ultimately for..."
]

More demands. And on top of all that, a baby. Then, as if the timing couldn't be worse, a fire swept through their small, one-bedroom apartment, destroying all their earthly possessions. Without insurance, the young Chapman family's financial future was on shaky ground. For three months they lived with friends, sleeping on the floor and wondering how they were going to make it. "It was the first time in my life," Steven would say later, "when I didn't have everything under control....that was when we started learning that Jesus wasn't kidding when He said we would have trouble in this world and that Christians aren't exempt from that."

In 1989, the Chapmans had another child, Caleb, who at five weeks old was diagnosed with a life-threatening medical problem that required surgery. It was yet another difficult lesson for Steven and Mary Beth. "Giving our baby over to the operating team, and walking to the edge of the sterile zone...that was the hardest thing Steven and I have ever had to do," Mary Beth says of that experience. "...I'd take that fire all over again."

Thankfully, the blond-haired boy recovered completely, much to the delight of his anxious parents and four-year old sister, Emily. Within two years, in 1991, Emily and Caleb were presented with Will Franklin, another rambunctious blue-eyed boy who would join the chorus of joyful chaos around the Chapman home.

Over the years, Steven Curtis and Mary Beth have worked hard to keep their young family healthy and strong, going to great lengths to coordinate schedules—his professional calendar and the family calendar. They've made every effort to stay connected to their families, to their community, to their church family and to their friends. And anyone who has ever listened to Steven Curtis, the artist, on stage, can testify to the running theme of family pride. His music reflects both the joy and the

challenges of being a husband and father in a seemingly fatherless, broken-family world.

Reconciling the personal with the performer is not always easy, but on stage as in life, he has made a commitment to be honest and to keep the main thing, the main thing. "I'm so thankful that I have a wife who longs for normalcy, who really won't settle for anything less than our lives being as real as she can possibly make it," Steven says, of the key role Mary Beth has played in keeping their priorities in line. "I Will Be Here," one of Steven's most popular songs, was written in the wake of his own parent's divorce, after 28 years of marriage. The song emphasizes his enduring commitment to Mary Beth and the life they've been building together for many years.

The awards and the rewards of celebrity will come and go, Steven acknowledges again and again, but the main thing will always be his family.

Which popular country artist later recorded Chapman's "I Will Be Here" on his own album?

TRIVIA QUESTION

BILLY DEAN

The Chapmans,
having a Dickens of
a good time for
Yuletide 1995.

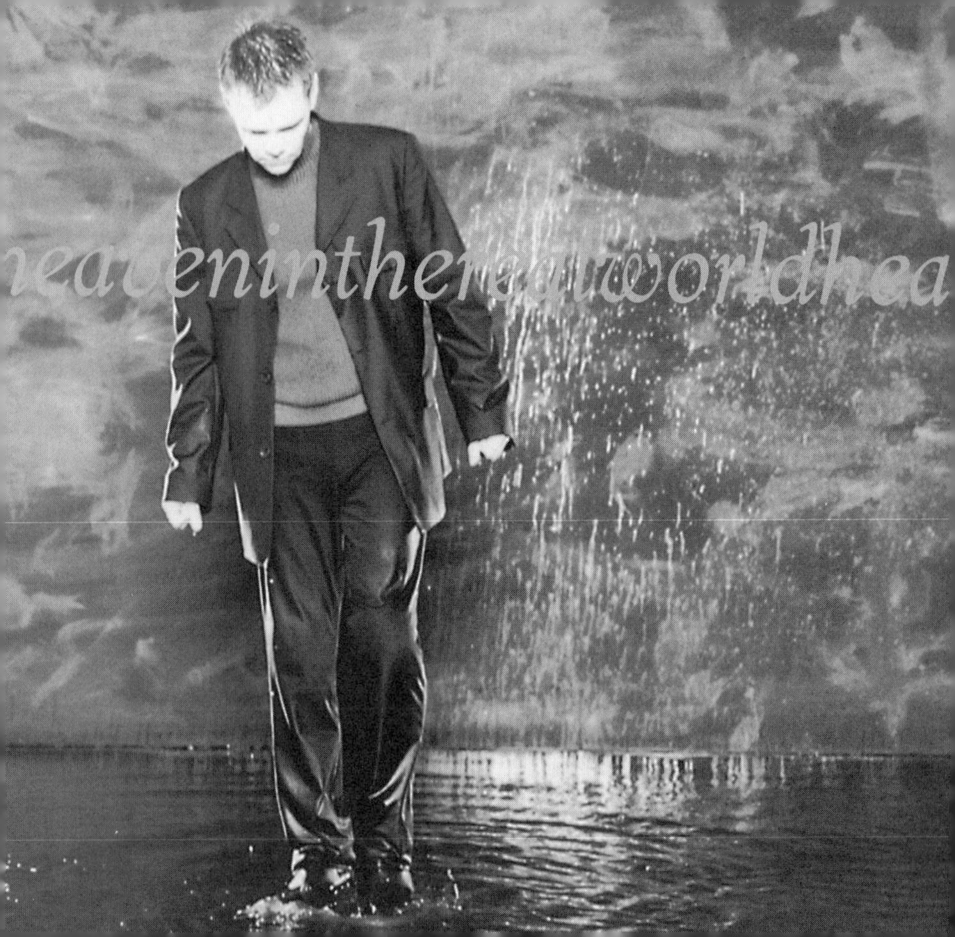
eaveninthe realworldhea

HEAVEN IN THE REAL WORLD

"*No better place on earth*

than the road that leads

to heaven, no better place

I'd rather be..."

FROM "NO BETTER PLACE" ON *FOR THE SAKE OF THE CALL* (1990)

HEAVEN

EARLY
CAREER

1987 was a banner year in Christian music. Twila Paris, Petra, Larnelle Harris, and Russ Taff were at the forefront of the scene. The year saw the controversial exit of music innovator Leslie Phillips, as well as the debut of such promising new acts as Kim Hill and Take 6. Categories for "Best Long Form Video" and "Best Short Form Video" were added to the Gospel Music Awards as the format grew in importance within Christian music. The "Christian music industry" was beginning to actually look like just that—a viable, marketing-driven industry.

And then there was Steve Chapman, fresh out of college, newly wed and signed to a recording contract with Sparrow Music. It was decided that, because Steve and Annie Chapman were already a well known music act, this Steve would use his full name as a stage name.

The road to stardom isn't always paved with gold. In fact, sometimes it isn't paved at all. In the early days, Steven definitely paid his dues, traveling from state to state and church to church, his borrowed sound equipment loaded up in the back of his Ford van and a U-Haul hooked up to carry the rest.

One of his first concerts was for the Baptist student union at Tennessee Technological University. He played his guitar in the lounge for an impressive crowd of 15. Another memorable gig was at a church in

Blue Earth, Minnesota, where the concert organizer was difficult to reach because he was literally out in the field all day, farming.

The equipment wasn't always adequate, and there were plenty of miscues, near accidents and last-minute problems to solve, but Steven's early years of touring sharpened his performance skills immensely, shaping him into the down-to-earth, vulnerable communicator he has become. The early years taught him what it takes to make the most of what you've got. Wherever he traveled and under whatever circumstances he played, he learned to connect with audiences from all walks of

"I write and sing songs and talk about
things that people can quickly latch on to.
It's not just a song with a good musical hook
and a catchy phrase; it's something they
can make their own...."

life. After the first two albums, Steven began to see a dramatic rise in his career. "I remember walking out on the stage in St. Louis, and there were 2,000 people in the audience. I thought I was in the wrong place. I was like, 'Who else is playing?'"

Along with the box office increase at concert performances, Steven's early career established him as a respected and accomplished songwriter, a "golden boy of Christian radio" whose music would do more than fly off the shelves. His music would touch lives.

In a 1990 interview in CCM MAGAZINE, Steven summed it up nicely:

"I write and sing songs and talk about things that people can quickly latch on to. It's not just a song with a good musical hook and a catchy phrase; it's something they can make their own....People come up to me after concerts and tell me that they feel I'm the sort of person they can talk to, that there's no kind of 'star' thing. And when I'm on stage, I really do feel that we're a family and I can share honestly with the audience."

That interview was Steven Curtis Chapman's first major interview in CCM MAGAZINE, the first time his boyish, "younger than his years" face would grace the cover. The first of many CCM covers featuring Steven.

"...when I 'm on stage, I really do feel that we're a family and I can share honestly..."

His first three albums, *First Hand*, *Real Life Conversations* and *More To This Life* spawned 12 Top Ten radio hits between them, six of those

making it to number one. "I Will Be Here," an expression of love and commitment, became an instant classic for weddings around the country. Album sales increased, as did concert attendance, and firmly established Steven as one of the most admired songwriters in Christian music.

Full House alumni—and SCC fans—Chelsea and Kirk Cameron greet Steven backstage after a concert.

Within two years of his debut, Steven Curtis Chapman was honored

with his first Grammy nomination for Best Gospel Performance for *Real*

Life Conversations, and his first Dove Award for Songwriter of the Year

and for Contemporary Song of the Year for "His Eyes." He had received

six Dove nominations, tying Amy Grant and Take 6 for the most bids.

A very solid beginning, indeed, but only the beginning.

Steven won a Dove Award in 1990 for Southern Gospel Recorded Song of the Year. What was the song and who recorded it?

TRIVIA QUESTION

"I CAN SEE THE HAND OF GOD," RECORDED BY THE CATHEDRA

MORE TO THIS LIFE

moretothislifemoretothislif

"*Saddle up your horses,*
We've got a trail to blaze,
to the wild blue yonder of
God's amazing grace.
Let's follow our leader into
the glorious unknown..."

FROM "THE GREAT ADVENTURE" ON *THE GREAT ADVENTURE* (1992)

MORE TO

THE
STORY
CONTINUES

With the advent of popularity and success, by 1991 Steven began to understand the importance of staying grounded, of deepening his understanding of the

Christian faith, what it means to be a disciple of Christ and the implications of this music career on his faith. Heavily impacted by Dietrich Bonhoeffer's classic, *The Cost of Discipleship*, Steven penned the songs for his most thematically focused album to date, *For the Sake of the Call*, which went on to win a Grammy Award for Best Pop Gospel Album in 1992.

With this album came the first opportunity to tour with a full band and full stage production. Steven began breaking new ground in his performances, adding a rock and roll energy that audiences enthusiastically embraced. As he became more and more aware of the performance

B.B. King, Jewel, Busta Rhyme and SCC team up in NYC with the prestigious assignment of announcing the year's Grammy Award nominees.

"What's most important is that I'm honest, real and vulnerable. And if I am, I'll make the music that I'm most naturally called to create."

possibilities that live instruments and production afforded, Steven's songwriting began to grow accordingly. Musically, *The Great Adventure* was a reflection of that growth, boosted by the collaborative efforts of popular artists such as Toby McKeehan of dcTalk, BeBe Winans, and Ricky Skaggs. And the album signaled Steven's venture into the video medium, which landed his rockin' country title cut on general market video outlets and on radio.

The excitement of his music and his career building, Steven turned his attention to addressing the hopelessness in our society. Responding

STEVEN CURTIS CHAPMAN

stevencurtischapman

IN *living* COLOR

The Chapman family
circa 1970
Steven, Herb Jr.,
Judy, and Herb Sr.

I WILL TESTIFY

Mr. Chapman goes to Washington.

THE TIES
HAVE IT

You've come a long
way, baby-face!—
25 years and only
the number of Doves
has changed.

SOMETHING TO
TALK ABOUT

Steven and rocker

Bonnie Raitt

Steven gives his all...
for the sake of the call.

THE CHAPMAN FAMILY

Will Franklin, Mary Beth, Steven, Emily and Caleb

The Chapmans meet the King of the Ice, Wayne Gretzky.

Holiday frolics with
the Chapman gang.

STEVEN CURTIS CHAPMAN

stevencurtischapman

IN *living* C O L O R

<————————————————————————————————>

to conversations with Chuck Colson, the head of Prison Fellowship, and James Dobson, he began to write songs to remind "the nation that forgot God" of the hope and peace found in Christ. *Heaven in the Real World* was the platinum-selling result, and in partnership with Prison Fellowship, Steven's tour promoted PF's Angel Tree Program, giving 100,000 Christmas gifts to children of incarcerated parents. His career began offering more than opportunities to make himself known. Steven began to see and take advantage of every opportunity to build the kingdom of Christ by proclaiming and defending the Truth and by living it.

"I don't need to change for the sake of change," he said, describing his artistic priorities in 1994. "What's most important is that I'm honest, real and vulnerable. And if I am, I'll make the music that I'm most natu- rally called to create. I won't ever stop stretching or looking for creative ways to freshen it up."

1995 and 1996 were years of great creative change for Steven. His first Christmas album, *The Music of Christmas*, became an instant classic and received yet another Grammy nomination. And *Signs of Life* ushered in an even more introspective Steven, with even more eclectic ideas and

Country superstar
Garth Brooks
swaps stage stories
with Steven.

SCC and producer
Brown Bannister
discuss *Speechless*...
with words

sounds than previously heard in his music. Packed with Scripture and produced by Brown Bannister, *Signs of Life* documented a transformation in the artist, a period of wrestling with the "nitty gritty of life" and rekindling his passion for God and for serving others. "The only thing that counts," he said of the lessons learned during this period, "is faith expressing itself through love." The 90-city tour that followed saw almost one half million people attend, and *Signs of Life*, as of this printing, has achieved gold status.

The more things change, the more they stay the same, the old adage says. And during this period of heightened success, that was definitely

true of Steven. Creatively, he was hitting new plateaus consistently,

[
"The only thing that counts is faith
expressing itself through love."
]

racking up the awards. Two more Grammy Awards in 1993 and 1994, 18

Dove Awards between 1991-1996, and many songwriter and readers' awards in between. *The Great Adventure* solidified Steven Curtis

Chapman's place among the key artists in Christian music, a position he

didn't—and still doesn't—take lightly.

TRIVIA QUESTION

In what year did
Steven win his first
Grammy award and
for which album?

IN 1992, FOR THE SAKE OF THE CALL

SPEECHLESS

peechlessspeechlesss peechl

> *"The river's deep, the river's wide, the river's water is alive, so sink or swim I'm divin' in..."*

FROM "DIVE" ON *SPEECHLESS* (1999)

FUTURE
WORLD

The view from the top, some would say, is the greatest view available. But what many don't take into consideration is that people at the top often lose sight of the real world, the values and ideas that got them to the top. Steven had always struggled to "keep the main thing, the main thing," but success, with all its obligations and pressures, had made the struggle even more complex.

At this stage in his career, stretching artistically meant not only doing one better than his last album, but also achieving the marketing success of younger artists like Jars of Clay and God's Property who were blowing the lid off the charts and flying off the shelves. For one who has always felt the need to please others as keenly as Steven has, that kind of intense pressure is almost overwhelming. As his *Greatest Hits* collection was

THE LONG AND WINDING ROAD

Steven records "The Walk" for his Greatest Hits album at the famed
Abbey Road Studio in London.

released in 1997, Steven began to question his role in Christian music.

"It's an ugly, weird thing [mixing] celebrity with the gospel," Steven said in a 1999 CCM interview, in reference to the thoughts he wrestled with while promoting and touring *Signs of Life*. "I've wondered many times if God really wired us to do what we're doing, the whole Christian celebrity thing. It's supposed to be about being a servant."

Weighed down by pressure and self-doubt, Steven made the decision to take some time off and catch his breath. Little did he know that his self-imposed sabbatical would be even more challenging than a career

Weighed down by pressure and self-doubt, Steven made the decision to take some time off and catch his breath.

Actor Robert Duvall joins SCC
for the making of the video for
"I Will Not Go Quietly."

running at breakneck speed. While there were some tremendous opportunities for Steven during this time—his song "I Will Not Go Quietly" made *The Apostle* soundtrack and the Chapman family traveled to South Africa—Steven was shaken by two tragic events. On December 1, 1997, his alma mater Heath High School in Paducah, Kentucky was the scene of a horrendous school shooting which gained national media attention. Then, a little over one month later, another unimaginable tragedy happened. The 8-year-old daughter of close family friends was killed in an automobile accident.

Steven and the boys
in the band Dive
into the music.

These tragedies, and the pain and grief that came with them, shook Steven to his core. He had never experienced this kind of loss and brokenness before. And God, in His providence and mercy, began to do a profound work in Steven's heart. "In that brokenness," Steven would later say, "I have felt tangible expressions of God's grace."

Awakening to the disruptive grace of God in the midst of great loss has had a tremendous impact on every aspect of Steven's life—husband, father, son and artist. He began to see with astonishment how powerful the grace of God is. Perhaps most significantly, he learned the importance

"*Speechless* is the artistic expression
of the pain and restlessness,
the joy and astonishment of this season."

of "letting go and letting God," of concentrating less on the expectations and pressures of life and placing his confidence in the One who makes all things possible.

Speechless is the artistic expression of the pain and restlessness, the joy and astonishment of this season. Musically, it is the most innovative, most confident project Steven has ever released. There is a tangible excitement and energy. "Because so many of these songs were written from such painful places, I thought the album would be darker," Steven said, "but God began to make all things new. To see all that newness come forward—not to put aside the pain of what I've learned, but to be able to say it with a sense of joy—has been an amazing gift for me."

In conjunction with the album, Steven co-authored a book with his pastor, Scotty Smith. *Speechless: Living in Awe of God's Disruptive Grace* (Zondervan) tells life-stories that bring the truth of grace to light. It is yet another new venture for Steven to broaden the outreach of his music and build the kingdom of God.

On tour, in the studio, or frolicking in the yard with his kids, these days find Steven Curtis Chapman more aware of how God's grace permeates the great rooms and small corners of his life. Awe-inspiring and ever true, this grace sustains both the man and the artist.

"To see all that newness... has been an amazing gift for me."

Thirty years have passed since little Stevie Chapman got his first guitar and began a great adventure on stages and stereos across the world. The guitars have changed,

the styles have changed, the hair has

changed—the world has changed.

But despite all the changes and all

the success he's achieved, Steven

THE THREE FACES OF STEVE

Fun in the photo booth.

Curtis Chapman has managed what most celebrities can not. While his 38 Dove Awards gather dust, he's still the kind-hearted, considerate and humble guy his mom and dad hoped he'd be. He's more than just an artist; he's a nice guy. A really nice guy.

DISCOGRAPHY

I n 12 years, Steven Curtis Chapman has

released 11 albums, including a collec-

tion celebrating ten years of recording, as well

as four music videos. To own all of them is to

see just how many different hair styles a man

can have. Oh, and you'll also hear just how well

one singer/songwriter can age musically.

1999 Speechless
(CD and co-author of the book)

1997 Greatest Hits

1997 The Walk (video)

1996 Signs of Life

1995 The Music of Christmas

1994 Heaven in the Real World

1993 The Live Adventure
(CD and video)

1992 The Great Adventure
(CD and video)

1990 Front Row (video)

1990 For the Sake of the Call

1989 More to This Life

1988 Real Life Conversations

1987 First Hand

COMPILATIONS

1998 The Prince Of Egypt
Nashville
Dreamworks SKG

1998 Songs 4 Life:
Embrace His Grace!
Songs 4 Life:
Renew Your Heart!
Songs 4 Life:
Lift Your Spirit!
Songs 4 Life:
Feel The Power!
Madacy Records

1998 WOW 1999: The
Year's 30 Top
Christian Artists
EMI Christian
Music Group 1998

1997 WOW 1998: The Year's 30 Top Christian Artists Chordant Music Group 1997

1996 WOW 1997: The Year's 30 Top Christian Artists [ECD] Sparrow Records 1996

1995 My Utmost For His Highest Word/Epic 1995

1995 WOW 1996: The Year's 30 Top Christian Artists Sparrow Records 1995

1994 Silver Anniversary Celebration Arrival

1994 Sparrow TV Dinners Sparrow Records

1994 Coram Deo II: People Of Praise Sparrow Records

1994 Promise Keepers: A Life That Shows Sparrow Records

1994 Giving You The Rest Of My Life... Sparrow Records

1994 Gospel Greats (1980-1992) Arrival

1992 Gospel Music Arrival

1991 Infinite Flight: A Sparrow Collection Sparrow Records

1990 I Will Be Here: 10 Contemporary Wedding Songs Sparrow Records

1988 Christmas Sparrow Records

The Greatest Love: A Wedding Collection Birdwing Records

Today's Top Christian Hits Arrival

ISN'T IT
—
DOVELY?

t only took one to break the news to Noah. But how many Doves does it take to make one man fly without benefit of wings? Good question. Dove Awards, among other awards and recognition, are practically old hat for Steven Curtis Chapman. Here's how the numbers line up!

Total Dove Awards
38

Record setting amount of Dove nominations at one time
10

Dove Awards for Songwriter of the Year
9

Grammy nominations
7

Grammy wins
3

It is hard to believe, but Steven Curtis Chapman has written or co-written every song on each of his 11 albums. That adds up to a lot of music! And don't forget that for almost every song chosen for an album, Steven has written at least one or two more that didn't make the final cut. The following songs not only made the cut, they hit the top of the charts. No fewer than 32 songs—that's almost three songs a year over the span of his career so far. No small feat, even for such an accomplished songwriter.

1999 "Be Still and Know"
"Speechless"
"Dive"

1998 "I Will Not Go Quietly"

1997 "Not Home Yet"

1996 "Lord of the Dance"
"Let Us Pray"
"Hold on to Jesus"
"Signs of Life"
"Free"

1995 "Christmas Is All in the Heart"
"Sometimes He Comes
in the Clouds"

1994 "Heaven in the Real World"
"King of the Jungle"
"Dancing with the Dinosaur"
"The Mountain"
"Heartbeat of Heaven"

1993 "The Great Adventure"
"Where We Belong"
"Go There With You"
"Still Called Today"

1992 "For the Sake of the Call"
"When You Are a Soldier"
"No Better Place"
"Busy Man"
"What Kind of Joy"

1990 "More To This Life"
"I Will Be Here"
"Love You With My Life"
"Treasure Island"

1989 "His Eyes"
"My Turn Now"

LIGHTS
CAMERA
ACTION

Christian music's golden boy has a television friendly face. That much is true. Steven Curtis Chapman has taken his brand of well-crafted, heart-felt pop music to the airwaves many times. Perhaps you've caught a glimpse of him on...

Music City Tonight

CBS This Morning

CNN Headline News

60 Minutes

Extra!

Prime Time Country

A Musical Christmas at
Walt Disney World

Live ...With Regis and
Kathie Lee

The Sunday Today Show

E! Entertainment

CNN Showbiz

Above: Steven joins Regis and Kathie Lee...Live and left: with sisters Ashley and Wynonna Judd.

BETCHA' DIDN'T KNOW...

betcha didn't knowbetcha

Steve Chapman only used his full name because there

was already a Steve Chapman in Christian music—

Steve and Annie Chapman were Christian music artists

in the early to mid '80s when SCC started out, and the

world wasn't large enough for another Steve Chapman.

"Curtis Chapman" was one of the options considered.

Steven's favorite cereal is Grapenuts.

———————

The first SCC-penned song that was ever recorded by a national artist was "Built to Last" by the Imperials.

———————

His first car? 1971 Camaro.

———————

Sandi Patty, Charlie Daniels, and Glen Campbell have all recorded Steven's songs.

Top: Steven with Reba McEntire and Gary Chapman

Above: Steven and Southern Belle Dixie Carter.

Steven's just as famous for consistently being late.

His favorite hymn? "Turn Your Eyes Upon Jesus."

The first album he owned, he won from a radio station: Andrae Crouch's *Live in London*.

In addition to his work at Opryland USA, Steven cut his musical teeth singing jingles and vocal tracks.

Steven is very missions-minded and has considered becoming a missionary.

CONTACT INFORMATION

ontactcontactcontactcont

You can write to Steven Curtis Chapman at
P.O. Box 150156, Nashville, TN 37215

---

or visit Steven on the web at
www.scchapman.com

WWW.SCCHAPMAN.COM

gotchacovered!

Steven Curtis Chapman
has graced the cover of
CCM MAGAZINE no less
than 9 times—making
him one of CCM's most
"covered" artists!

July 1988

April 1993

October 1996

April 1990

July 1992

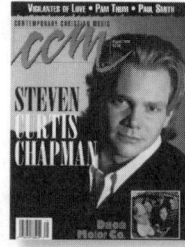

December 1993

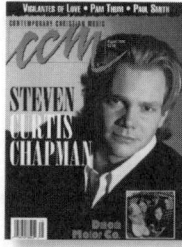

August 1994

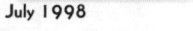

July 1998

July 1999

P9WH

To subscribe, call **1-800-210-7584** or visit **ccmmagazine.com**

Just $21.95 for 12 jam-packed issues.

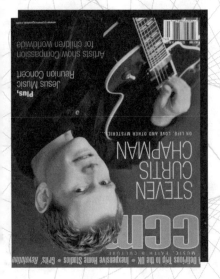

Get the latest information on the hottest artists, songs and top albums

Read honest reviews of new releases to help you buy wisely

Learn up-to-date concert information for your area